My Crow, Hoppy

My Crow, Hoppy

A True Story For All Ages

Joy Johns

Copyright © 2009 by Joy Johns.

ISBN:	Hardcover	978-1-4415-4086-7
	Softcover	978-1-4415-4085-0

All rights reserved. No part of this book may be reproduced or transmitted in any form or by any means, electronic or mechanical, including photocopying, recording, or by any information storage and retrieval system, without permission in writing from the copyright owner.

Names, characters, places and incidents are based on author's experiences. Images contained in this book have been purchased from www.clipart.com.

This book was printed in the United States of America.

To order additional copies of this book, contact:
Xlibris Corporation
1-888-795-4274
www.Xlibris.com
Orders@Xlibris.com
49447

Dedication

To my cousin Bobbie, who has been a source of inspiration and strength. She loves all creatures, whether tame or wild, and spends much of her time feeding and caring for all the critters that share her lake property. Her favorites are the wild birds and raccoons. She also has adopted many stray cats which have been abandoned. Although a widow, she is never lonely or sad, with so many friends to brighten her days.

And,

To Terri, the proprietor of my home town pet shop, who is always available to assist pet owners with the care and well being of their critters, usually free of charge . . . whether she sold them or not. She is treasured in this community as much as the pastors, doctors, teachers or government leaders. Terri knows that the bond between pets and owners is a source of healing that rivals modern medicine. Thus, she is always there to help foster this love.

INTRODUCTION

I have been waiting to tell this tale for over 50 years, a true story of events which occurred during my twelfth year. I have hesitated to write my story for so long out of fear that I would be accused of copying the theme of *The Yearling*, a famous book by Marjorie Rawlings. She tells the story of Jody, a young boy who must part with his beloved pet deer, causing such deep sorrow that he runs away and almost dies. He must leave childhood innocence behind and face the challenges of growing up. Like Jody, I had to part with my most prized possession, my beloved pet. However, my special friend was not a deer, but a crow. Although you may dislike sad stories, please read on, because you will be not only disappointed, but also delighted!

CHAPTER 1

I was an only-child, a very lonely and isolated little girl. In 1949 I turned seven and moved with my parents to a small town near St. Louis, Missouri. There were no other children my age in our family or in this new neighborhood. To compensate, my parents brought several pets into our home. First, they tried a cat. He was a fluffy longhaired Tom we called Frosty, who was very independent and insisted on prowling around far from home. He wasn't much fun. Then they bought Nicky for my tenth birthday. He was a feisty terrier, very noisy and nervous. He barked a lot and chased his tail, but was not a great companion. In fact, I found both the dog and the cat to be quite boring!

That was the trouble. Up to this point, I was not only lonely, but also very bored. My poor parents didn't know what to do with me. My teachers said I was very smart, but I remained sullen and withdrawn, even at school. So my parents next tried piano lessons and dancing lessons and skating lessons—even camp and Girl scouts! But nothing helped. I was still bored. Nothing seemed to spark my imagination or sense of adventure. So, I just sat under the big elm tree in our back yard and stared up at the clouds, lost in a child's world of daydreams.

Then, it happened.

CHAPTER 2

Shortly after my twelfth birthday, Dad arrived home early from work one day with a big sheepish grin from ear to ear.

"What's up," I wondered. Then I noticed a brown cardboard box, tied loosely with string, tucked under his arm. He carefully set it down at my feet. Holes were punched in the top, and I could hear strange noises coming from inside. "Now what's he brought home to amuse me?" I smirked to myself. I carefully pulled away the string, but before I could open the flaps, a black creature burst up into the air. Startled, I fell back on the floor, and the thing landed on my head. I felt something sharp poking my hair. I reached up with my hands and gripped something fluffy. When I brought my hands down to my lap, there sat a big black bird!

"It's a baby crow!" Dad proudly announced.

I wondered how a "baby" could be a foot tall! This strange creature stared at me intently for awhile, and then jumped down on the floor and began hopping all around the room like he had springs on his feet. Thus came his name, "Hoppy."

"How did you catch him? Where did you find him? Can I keep him? How do I feed him? Will he bite? Where is his mother? Why did you bring him home?" And on and on came the onslaught of questions to my bewildered parent.

"Now, wait a minute. Slow down, and I will explain everything." He proceeded to tell his story of how he brought Hoppy home in the brown box.

Dad was a construction worker. His company was clearing land to begin construction of a big shopping center. They were about to take down a grove of trees, when he noticed a big nest in the top of the tallest oak. Then a big crow came sailing down and screeched and flapped over the workers heads. My dad knew this was the mother crow, trying to protect her young in the nest. In fact, my dad knew quite a lot about crows and most other wildlife, because he was born and raised in the Arkansas wilderness. He grew up on a farm, walked barefoot three miles to school everyday, and had many wild creatures for pets. I had heard countless stories about his pet snakes, wolves, groundhogs, squirrels, and crows. So, when he continued to explain how Hoppy ended up on our kitchen floor, I was confident that he would know just what to do.

He knew the tree would come down and the young birds in the nest would die. So he climbed up and carefully brought the whole nest down, while the mother crow dived at his head. There were three in the nest. He gave two away to the other workers, and brought Hoppy home to me.

Dad told me that he had learned back on the farm that crows were easy to domesticate and made very amusing pets, as they were "full of the devil" and extremely smart. He said all one had to do was to retrieve the fledgling bird just before time to leave the nest, bring it home, feed it once, and it was yours forever.

"Well, what does this strange creature eat? How do I feed him, especially since he's just a baby?" I asked in dismay.

"Oh, that's the easiest part," my Dad assured me. "Just open a can of dog food and hold it in your hand while he sits on your arm."

I proceeded to do just that. Hoppy stuck his whole head down in the can. I thought he would never come up for air. He gobbled down almost the whole can. And sure enough, he never tried to fly away or leave me after that first feeding.

CHAPTER 3

During that summer of my twelfth year, our adventures together were unbelievable! In no time, Hoppy was flying all around, but he preferred riding on my shoulders or on the handlebars of my bike. He rode everywhere with me, his sleek black feathers glowing in the sun and rippling in the wind. Sometimes he would nestle down in my bike basket and take a quick nap. He cackled and cooed, making funny crow sounds as we sped down the road.

Some people say you should split a crows tongue so they will learn to talk like a parrot, but Dad claimed this was just an old wives tale. He claimed that crows could out-talk parrots any day . . . . no tongue splitting required! Besides, I would never let anyone do that to Hoppy. He could almost talk, anyway! When flying around above me, he would omit "Caw-Caw" calls that sounded like the other wild crows in the area. But, when perched on me or nearby, we carried on our own conversations in our own secret code and communicated just fine! Sometimes he would jabber sweet-nothings into my ear. "Hi!" or

"Come on!" or "Love you!" or "Yum Yum!" were some of his favorite messages.

After my new pet had learned to fly, Mom no longer allowed him to come inside with me. Nevertheless, no matter where Hoppy was, when I went outside to play, all I had to do was call him by name. Instantly he came gliding down out of the sky, lighting gently on my shoulder. I don't know for sure where he went when I wasn't around, but it must not have been very far, because he always appeared within seconds. I do know that he slept in the big elm tree right outside my bedroom window.

Hoppy enjoyed many other summer activities besides bike riding. His favorite was playing in the plastic wading pool which I had bought just for him. He loved to flop around and get me all wet. We would sit for hours and play games in the water. He would chase bugs and water toys for as long as I would stay with him.

He also liked to sit on the patio in the cool evenings and chat with the whole family. When Mom and I crossed our legs, Hoppy jumped up on our feet and jabbered away long into the evenings. Sometimes it was hard to get a word in edgewise. He loved ice cubes, so he would stick his head down into our ice-tea glasses and grab a cube. Then he would hold it in his feet and crack it with hard jabs of his sharp beak.

Another summer time activity my crow relished was our sun-tanning sessions. Whenever I carried my beach towel and radio into the back yard, Hoppy cackled with glee. He would come hopping across the yard to stake out his place on the towel. Sometimes he swayed to the rock music, flapping his wings and bowing his head up and down in time to the beat. But, usually he stretched out on the ground by my head, spread out his wings, cooed in my ear, and helped me soak up the sun. What I didn't like was when he jumped up on my sunburned back and pranced around with his sharp claws!

Another of his favorite tasks was my most dreaded duty, weeding the yard. At first, Hoppy just watched me as I lumbered through this dreaded assignment. He hopped all around me as he tried to figure out a way to help me get this job done so we could go for a bike ride.

Then I noticed him sitting back on his tail with a big yellow dandelion in his bill, pulling with all his might. He flopped his wings and suddenly fell backwards, but the weed lost! He hopped proudly over to my feet and proceeded to drop his golden prize into my half-full bucket. From then on, I completed my weed job in half the time!

CHAPTER 4

As we shared so many adventures during my twelfth summer, I learned many things about crows. For example, they love shinny objects. Hoppy was always on the outlook for some new bright trinkets to add to his collection, most of which he hid up in the gutter above my bedroom window. I had to climb up on a ladder at the end of each day to see what new treasures he had added to his stash. One day my dad couldn't find his favorite cigarette lighter, a silver souvenir he had brought back from a vacation in Mexico. Well, you guessed it; we found it up in the gutter that night, along with a fork, a pearl button, a silver key, some nails, a ring, and a screwdriver.

Sometimes this clever thief hid his treasures in one of Mom's big clay pots. The opening was big enough for him to stick his head into, but I never saw him retrieve anything from this vessel. One day I saw him wearing something shinny around his neck. I was inside peeking out my bedroom window, so I couldn't tell what it was. He hopped over to the clay pot and stuck his head in all the way. When he came back up, the object was no longer around his neck. I ran out to the garden to see what this bandit had dropped into his treasure pot . . . . my favorite bracelet! Thus, I learned not to leave valuables just lying around. Mom also had a smaller brass pot which had a very narrow neck, too small to stick his head into. However, he seemed to be fascinated by this shinny container, hopping around and around it, sometimes depositing small seeds and pebbles. I guess this was just a game.

I quickly learned how witty and clever my new friend was. For example, when I gave him walnuts or pecans for snacks, he would fly over our driveway, drop them and leave them lying there. Then, as soon as the car pulled out and ran over the nuts, he swooped down to retrieve the goodies, avoiding all the work of having to crack them. Sometimes, when I gave Hoppy bread crumbs or chips, instead of eating them, he would fly over the neighbor's pond and drop them. Then when small minnows surfaced to take the bait, he snatched his prize! This crow loved to go fishing.

Hoppy also had a sharp sense of humor. He loved to sit on the neighbor's porch and play tricks, such as ringing the doorbell. Then when they opened the door, he would laugh, "Ha, ha . . . Ha, ha!" Also, when the mailman delivered mail to the road boxes, Hoppy would soon land and pry open these treasure chests with his beak, cawing with glee when finding something fun to hide in his stash up in our back gutter. If nothing else, he shredded up the paper items and tossed them to the ground! I don't know whether to attribute these pranks to humor or mischief, but Hoppy and I thought they were great fun, even if no one else did!

My crow seemed to have a great imagination. When I was not around to entertain him, he would think up all kinds of things to do. One day I left my sneakers outside on the porch. When I came back out to put them on, the laces were missing, from both shoes. "Who did this?" I mused. Then I knew. Glancing up into Hoppy's elm tree I spied all the laces hanging from the branches. He had created Christmas in July with his very own Christmas tree!

He also liked to open containers, always hoping their would be something fun inside. Whenever my dad left a pack of his cigarettes outside, Hoppy grabbed them and flew off to one of the branches in his elm tree. There he proceeded to rip open the pack and shred up the contents, making a shower of confetti. One day Dad grabbed the hose and sprayed Hoppy with cold water as he was making confetti up in the tree. After that, he left Dad's cigarettes alone. But nothing else was off limits to Hoppy's inquiring mind. Once I saw him land on a can of band aids, which was too big for him to carry off. But he pried off the lid and emptied the contents all over the ground, proceeding to tear open every single band aid. Curiosity may have killed the cat, but not the crow!

Hoppy didn't seem to have any fear of other pets or animals. He would fuss at the squirrels in the back yard, swooping down and pecking their heads and grabbing at their tails. These pesky little rodents always retreated quickly. One day I saw him hopping around our cat's food dish, which was full of treats. He flew down for a sample, but old Frosty ran over to protect his meal. Hoppy flew up on a chair, but when Frosty tried to eat, he flew back down behind him, grabbed on to the tip of his bushy tail, and pulled and yanked, until Frosty gave up and left the dish all to Hoppy. I will never forget our old cat's look of distain as he peered around to see this bundle of black feathers playing tug-of-war with his tail! Many of our neighbors claimed that this thief regularly robbed their pets' outside food dishes. I wonder if he pulled on their tails?

The most significant thing I learned about Hoppy during our first few months together was that he made the rules. For example, he invented bird-ball. We played by his rules. After stealing one of Frosty's small rubber balls, he flew with it to the picnic table and dropped it in front of me. Then he would roll it off the table with his beak. I had to try and catch it before it hit the ground. When I missed, he laughed with glee . . . "Caw, caw, caw . . . . Ha, ha!" That was a point for Hoppy. He always scored the most points.

Whenever we went bike riding, he set the schedule by letting me know when we were too far from home and when it was time to go back. Then my mindful companion would leap into the air and snatch my hat, flying towards home. Of course, I quickly followed.

When my demanding buddy wanted food or attention, he would perch up in his elm tree and caw loudly, raising such a ruckus that his wishes were soon granted. But, if that didn't work, he would hop onto the dinner bell which Dad had mounted on the back porch. If we still hadn't answered his demands, he pulled the chain with his beak and made the loud bell cling and clang till we came running. I don't know how long he must have continued this clatter when we weren't home, but I bet the neighbors had to get some ear plugs!

Thus, I learned that you can't own a pet crow . . . . They tend to own you!

CHAPTER 5

Now, I don't want you to believe life with this comical bird was all fun and games! He did get me into some tense situations.

It was close to the end of August, almost time for school to restart, when Dad noticed that Hoppy was digging at himself with his beak and claws. Upon closer inspection, we determined that he was infested with mites. This itching became so intense that Dad decided to spray him with DDT, a poison bug spray that has long since been banned. This was a grave mistake.

In a short time my poor crow became extremely ill. He wouldn't eat or drink or fly. We took him to our veterinarian, but he said there was nothing we could do but watch him closely.

For the first time Mom let me bring Hoppy into the house, down into the cool, dark basement. My sick friend sat on the back of a wooden chair, while I sat on the floor right next to him. He continued to refuse to eat or drink. As each day passed, he grew weaker and weaker, his wings drooping low and his eyes almost shut. He made soft cooing sounds when he heard my pleas: "Please Hoppy, don't die. You're my very best friend. Don't worry, I won't leave you, not for one minute!" And I didn't, except for restroom breaks. I didn't eat either.

Finally, after a week of this suffering, Hoppy let me give him some sips of water through an eyedropper. Next, His eyes gradually opened, his wings perked up, and he began to eat. He was going to be okay. Tears of relief rolled down my cheeks. Soon my best friend was jabbering and cackling and flapping his wings. This was his way of telling me that he was ready for some action. He jumped down to the concrete basement floor and proceeded to check out his new surroundings. I sat down on his wooden chair and brushed my hair as I watched him walk around. Finding nothing of interest, he came over and jumped up into my lap. He loved for me to rub him softly with my hairbrush.

    Suddenly he darted over to the stairs and hopped up to the back door. He had enough of the confinement of life on the inside. Hoppy missed the freedom and fun of his outside world. So I opened the door, and he instantly flew up to his favorite branch in the old elm tree. He spent the next several hours chasing away all the squirrels that had taken over his tree, nipping their ears and jerking their tails. The next day we went for one of our long bike rides, chatting about the upcoming week's adventures.

CHAPTER 6

Much to our dismay, summer vacation was coming to an end, and I had to spend more and more time away from Hoppy. His mischievous ways soon began to get him into all sorts of trouble.

On the first day of school he attempted to follow me. My inseparable friend had watched me walk to the bus stop, where he perched high in the trees across the street. He tried to interrupt this early morning meeting with my schoolmates with jealous caws. Then, just as the bus pulled up, it began to rain. We all boarded quickly to get out of the downpour. Before the bus began to move, the lady driver started to scream in terror! I pushed my way forward to see what was happening. I couldn't believe my eyes. Hoppy was swinging back and forth on the outside of the windshield on the wipers! He had attached himself with his claws and was hanging on for dear-life, swishing to and fro on high-speed! I guess he thought he was going to go to school with me one way or another. Anyway, he rode the wipers for many minutes, like a cowboy in a rodeo. The kids cheered with glee, while the terrified driver continued to holler. Finally, Hoppy gave up and flew off towards home, unharmed but frustrated. Needless to say, we were late for school. Rumor had it that the novice bus driver quit her job the next day, which must be so because we never saw her again.

As Hoppy spent more and more time alone, he managed to get into some precarious predicaments. One weekend went by without a sign of him. I called and called, but Hoppy was no where. He had never been gone this long before. This was the first time he didn't appear at the sound of my voice. Just as I was about to panic, our front door bell rang. I opened the door to a strange sight. A neighbor from three blocks away was standing on our front porch, holding a huge ball of orange knitting yarn the size of a basketball. "Here's your danged Crow!" he angrily shouted at me. Then he proceeded to describe the horror of that morning's events.

His wife had been enjoying some quiet time out on their patio, knitting a sweater. Well, Hoppy spotted the bright pair of silver knitting needles, and swooped known to grab them. But his claws became all tangled in the yarn. The lady almost had a heart attack as this big black bird flopped and squawked and unraveled all her hard work. Her husband tried and tried to get Hoppy untangled, but to no avail. He finally just rolled all the yarn up around this black demon and brought him back to me in a big ball of bright, orange yarn!

CHAPTER 7

The neighbors began complaining more and more. I have already revealed how Hoppy would ring door bells and raid the mailboxes, but these pranks escalated with my absence. Many folks soon suspected that the neighborhood was haunted. Doorbells kept ringing for blocks around, but no one was there. Also, missing mail was becoming a serious problem. After all, this could be a Federal matter! We soon discovered that the culprit was Hoppy. However, all this was just a way he had to amuse himself in my absence. I suspect that he really liked to aggravate the neighbors. After all, it is said that crows are by nature quite mischievous.

Back then it was customary to hang wet clothes on lines outside so they could dry in the fresh air. I don't remember anyone having clothes dryers. So, the neighbor ladies were quite upset when their clean clothes kept falling on the ground. Next they discovered that their clothespins were missing. You guessed it. When I climbed up to the gutter to see what new items Hoppy was hoarding, I found over fifty clothespins! If this were not bad enough, sometimes he would walk around in the mud and then land on their clean white sheets and towels and leave muddy crow prints all up and down the lines! I think some of these housewives were planning a new recipe for crow stew!

Also, It was one thing when this devil bird stole balls from our cat, but when he started playing this game at the nearby golf course, tempers flared! He loved to perch in a big oak tree overlooking the putting green which was surrounded by a pond. Hoppy watched patiently as the golfers eyed up their putts. Without warning he would swoop down and grab the little white ball. Then, he then would soar over the pond and drop the ball right in the middle. The golfers waved their hats in anger, and sometimes threw their clubs up into the air, screaming many unprintable obscenities . . . tarnishing the reputation of this dignified game!

One day in late autumn, the neighbors across the street came home to a horrible sight. As soon as they pulled into their driveway, they heard their dog Rusty yelping and howling in the back yard. Rusty was an aging pooch who wouldn't hurt a flea. They rushed around to the back and discovered that Hoppy was hanging on to this sweet dog's long fur with his claws, swinging back and forth, as the poor tormented dog ran around the yard. One such episode would have been cause enough for dismay, but Hoppy found the torment of this poor old dog so entertaining that he hitched a ride every chance he got, sometimes several times a day. Well, it wasn't long before we received a vet bill for Rusty's nervous breakdown!

Hoppy also harassed the little girl who lived next door. She was an only child like me, but a few years younger. However, once in a while we liked to play together. Well, Hoppy did not relish sharing his time with me one bit. So, he proceeded to attack this poor child every time he spied her outdoors. He would swoop down swiftly and pounce upon her head, pecking away with much ferocity, while making ear piercing screams, sounding like a ghoulish vampire. The little girl retreated in tears every time. Hoppy also liked to sabotage her wading pool. When no one was looking, he would gather up pine cones, bugs, worms and all sorts of unpleasant things. Then he would fly over the pool like a B-52, shouting what sounded like "Bombs Away!" Sometimes, her pool had to be emptied and refilled several times a day!

Perhaps what upset folks the most was Hoppy's gardening hobby. He loved to replant. As soon as our fellow gardeners planted something, he would sweep down and scratch up the dirt and eat the freshly planted seeds. Or, this bandit would sometimes steal the seeds and drop them into our yard or into Mom's pots. Thus, I often found corn and beans and all kinds of strange plants sprouting up around our house.

Many proclaimed that this black demon was becoming evil, maybe even a threat to the safety of the neighborhood pets and children. Nevertheless, I knew that Hoppy was just bored and lonesome, and maybe a bit jealous. Whatever, I found all these pranks to be quite hilarious. No matter how depressing my day at school was, Hoppy always made me laugh by the end of the day.

CHAPTER 8

As the school year progressed and winter approached, Hoppy's escapades created more and more havoc. Halloween was coming soon, and my pesky friend was having a ball attacking and tearing up the decorations, especially the scarecrows. He pecked out their eyes, noses and lips, and hid them in our gutter. I also found buttons and shoe laces, a neck scarf and even an old hat in his trick-or-treat stash.

Hoppy also perched on the pumpkins and cawed loudly, trying to spook the neighbors. He especially liked the jack-o-lanterns. He loved to peck and chew up the faces, making the holes bigger so he could stick his head inside and eat the goodies. I thought Hoppy's faces were always better than the originals, but the neighbors were furious that all their hard work was destroyed . . . especially since there was going to be a contest and prizes for the best faces. But, it was one of Hoppy's altered creations that ended up on the front page of the paper as one of the finalists This pumpkin looked like it had been carved by a chainsaw, but the judges thought it was a piece of art and awarded it the first place price of $500! The owner of this pumpkin was no longer angry at Hoppy. In fact, he decided to share his winnings with this creative trick-or-treater. Dad split these winnings with the folks who suffered loses from Hoppy's pranks. Most of the other neighbors, however, were not so pleased. I think they were just jealous.

Even though it was past his bedtime, I took this prankster trick-or-treating with me. He loved ringing the doorbells. He flapped his wings and screeched loudly to appear scary. I was dressed as a witch, but Hoppy was just himself. The nice neighbors gave me double treats . . . one for me and one for Hoppy!

CHAPTER 9

I began to look forward to Fridays so that I could keep a watchful eye on this mischief maker and keep him out of trouble. We were always too busy having fun to get into trouble. However, one Friday in early November, as I departed the school bus, I knew something was wrong. There was a row of strange vehicles in our driveway.

It turned out that several of the disgruntled neighbors had complained to the authorities about Hoppy's misdemeanors. The wild life commissioner, the sheriff, and a humane society officer were meeting with my dad. It was illegal to keep a pet crow, but they decided that, since we had not caged this wild bird or clipped his wings, we had not broken any laws. However, they also proclaimed that he had become a public nuisance. Thus, they ordered us to get rid of him. They gave us a choice: either we would find a way to keep Hoppy from annoying the neighbors or they would take matters into their own hands. One way or another, this could mean the demise of Hoppy.

At first I was amused. How could grown-ups get so out of joint by the minor infractions of a comical and loving pet? Surely they were not serious!

Yes, they were!

Well, my dad thought about it long and hard. He knew that we could not cage this bird or keep him inside. The only solution was to release him out in the wild, far away, so he couldn't find his way back to us. The prospects of subjecting my beloved pet to this cruel fate filled me with horror. I could not bear to think of life without Hoppy. In an instant I decided to run away and try to save my best friend.

Since it was Friday, I had all weekend to work on this project, but I knew I had no time to waste. Dad could decide to take Hoppy at any moment. So, after supper, while my parents were busy cleaning up, I went outside and invited my friend to go for one of our evening bike rides.

As we sped down the road, I had no idea where to go or what to do. I was in a daze. Then an idea popped into my thoughts. I remembered an old deserted homestead in the middle of a big field on the outskirts of town. Hoppy and I often rode by it, but never stopped to investigate, even though the old, rusty gate was half open. The property was condemned and posted with warning and keep-out signs. There were many spooky rumors of weird happenings at this abandoned address. Some of the towns people said there had been a murder here. Many claimed that the old place was haunted, but they may have made up this story to keep kids like me away and out of danger. In any case, no one I knew had the courage to explore past the front gate.

I turned into the dirt road, now so grown up with weeds that the path was almost invisible. I hopped off my bike and proceeded on foot, with Hoppy perched on my shoulder. He cackled with excitement, happy to be starting a new adventure.

The field was a jungle of waist high brush and vines. I could barely see the old house. After what seemed forever, we arrived at the front yard, now covered in debris from the dilapidated building that had once been someone's home. Half of the house was on the ground. The windows were all boarded up or covered with shutters. The front porch was still intact, so we gingerly climbed up and looked around. There were no doors or windows, so I couldn't leave Hoppy out on the porch. The front door to the house was in place and slightly ajar. As I pushed it open, a loud creepy squeak echoed from within. Was it the door or something or someone lurking inside? Since all the windows were covered and darkness was setting in, I could barely see inside. Having no flashlight, I did not dare to enter. How could I leave Hoppy in such a scary setting? I thought about the alternative and knew there was only one choice. So I gently set him on the floor just inside the door. I told him I would be back early in the morning, that all would be just fine. He didn't seem to be afraid or upset, so I shut the door, ran back to my bike and peddled furiously, trying to reach home before dark.

My parents were worried and demanded to know where I had been. I told them that Hoppy and I had gone for a final bike ride, but that he had suddenly flown off, joining a flock of wild crows. I claimed to have called and called after him, but to no avail. I never had lied before, but would now do anything to save my dear friend. I don't think my dad believed my tale, but he questioned me no farther.

I went directly to bed, saying that I didn't feel well, but I didn't sleep any. I stayed awake all night planning my next steps in Hoppy's escape. Visions of what supplies we would need swirled around in my head . . . . a flashlight, candles, food and water for Hoppy, some snacks for me, an extra sweater, and my sleeping bag. So, I sneaked out of my room in the middle of the night, filled up my backpack with supplies and went outside to find a place of safety for my bundle, out of my parents' sight. I managed to make it back inside to my room, undetected. The next morning at breakfast, I asked my parents if I could be excused to go look for Hoppy. They seemed to think this was a good idea, but that I should wear a jacket, as it was chilly this time of year. Thus, I quickly jumped on my bike and rode to the bush where I had hidden my pack. Then off I raced to see if Hoppy had made it safely through the night.

CHAPTER 10

As soon as I arrived at the front porch entrance, I called out to Hoppy. He immediately answered me back. I eased open the rickety wooden door and peered cautiously around inside, but didn't see my friend. Then he uttered another joyful screech from above. There he was up on a high ceiling beam. He flew down to my shoulder and cooed softly into my ear and rubbed my cheek with his bill.

After giving him food and water, we set out to explore the ancient house. Most of the floor boards were loose and made strange noises as we walked around on tip-toes. The sun was shinning brightly outside, but little light came in through the closed shutters. So I shinned my flashlight to chase away the spooky shadows.

This first room appeared to have been a family room. There was a fireplace, a faded old sofa with all the stuffing hanging out and a wooden rocker. Everything was covered in cobwebs. Then we came to a long, dark hallway. At the end was a spiral staircase leading upstairs and a kitchen. The rest of the bottom floor was in ruins, as the roof and second story had caved in long ago.

We decided to explore the kitchen first. There was a sink, an old refrigerator with no door and a wood stove. In one corner was a wooden table but no chairs. I heard a noise coming from a cabinet over the sink. What could it be? Hoppy didn't seem afraid, as he flew over to investigate, landing on the sink faucet. My heart was in my mouth as I slowly pulled open the cabinet door. Out jumped a chipmunk! He quickly scurried out of sight.

Now it was time to check out the upstairs. The old staircase seemed solid, so I continued my upward climb, with Hoppy on my shoulder. At the top was another window with closed shutters. However, several pieces of wood were missing, so the sun peeked in to brighten up our exploration.

There were four closed doors leading off the hallway, which I assume were bedrooms. I had noticed an outhouse in the side yard, so I concluded there were no bathrooms inside. I didn't dare open any doors on the side of the house which had caved in. The other two rooms were empty, so we didn't venture inside. After all, with all the loose flooring, we could have fallen through. So, we decided to carefully make our way back downstairs. I concluded that this old house was a safe enough hiding place for my Hoppy . . . at least temporarily. I was checking for holes in the walls or loose ceiling boards where he could escape, but I didn't see any.

Once back in the front room, I sat down in the wooden rocker, as I feared what might be lurking inside the dirty old sofa. Hoppy flew up to his rafter, which he seemed to enjoy. I told him that I must soon go back home, before my parents began to worry about my whereabouts. I didn't want them to come looking for me. However, I assured my special friend that I would be back later that day. After putting him out some more food and water, I hurried back home.

Sure enough, my parents were about ready to come looking for me. They asked if I had seen any sign of Hoppy. Of course, I told them that I looked high and low, but he was nowhere to be found. My dad concluded that he must have taken up with the wild crows. Acting relieved, I inquired if I could spend the night with one of my friends who was having a slumber party. Thinking that this would be a good diversion in this time of unhappy events, they quickly agreed. So I pretended to pack my overnight bag, but instead of clothes, I jammed in snacks, bottles of water and a portable radio. After lunch I was off again to visit Hoppy, but this time I would spend the night.

CHAPTER 11

When I arrived at our hideout, I called out for Hoppy as soon as my bike hit the ground. But this time he failed to answer me. I grabbed my overnight bag and ran up to the front door and burst into the front room. But Hoppy was not up on his rafter. I thought that maybe he had escaped. I quickly looked all around. Then I spied him up on the staircase railing, all the way up at the top. He refused to fly down to me, even after I put some of his favorite treats in his bowl, which was still full from that morning. He hadn't eaten a bite. He was all puffed up and wouldn't utter a word to me. I wondered if he might be sick.

    I wanted Hoppy to come down and play with me. I thought maybe the radio would entice him down because he loved to sway and dance to music in the back yard at home. I found a music station playing the top hits. I danced around and around the room, skipping across the loose boards, but Hoppy ignored me. Next I tried sitting in the wooden rocker, thinking that maybe he would fly down to me. I was so tired from so little sleep that I soon dozed off. When I awoke, it was almost dark. I lit some candles and turned on the flashlight. The room took on a cozy glow, but my stubborn bird still refused to move. My stomach growled with hunger, so I made some crackers and cheese, one of Hoppy's favorite dishes, but he still wouldn't budge. In fact, he was now tucking his head under his wing and standing on one foot. I guess it was past his bedtime.

I was so lonely and sad and worried that I decided to join him. I unrolled my sleeping bag over by the stairs to be near Hoppy. After blowing out the candles, I clicked on my flashlight and crawled into my bag and zipped it all the way up, keeping my light on.

Suddenly it dawned on me what must be wrong with Hoppy. Where I was keeping him was just as bad, if not worse, than a cage. When I was gone, he was in the dark and alone. This must be why he moved his perch up to the top of the stairs, where a bit more light came through the broken shutters. How he must miss the bright sunshine and his funny game of hiding shinny treasures in the gutter. However, at least in a cage at home, there would be light. We could set him out on the porch, or bring him inside where he would enjoy our company and the warmth of electricity. We could take him for car rides, on picnics, and to visit friends. I didn't see why this cage idea wouldn't work. We could have a small cage for outings, a giant cage for inside. Then I remembered . . . . It was against the law to keep wild birds such as crows caged. "There must be something we can do," I sobbed out loud. Tears rolled down my cheeks for hours, till I finally fell asleep.

When I awoke, my flashlight had burned out. I slowly unzipped my sleeping bag and peered up towards Hoppy. There he was, still at the top of the stairs on the railing, his head under his wing. I peeked through the shutters. The sun was bright and cheerful. If Hoppy had spent the night in his big elm tree, he would already be up and about, seeking adventure and fun. To test my theory, I opened the door wide and let in the warm light. Instantly, Hoppy flew down to my shoulder and rubbed my cheek with his head. Then he let out a loud caw-caw-caw, as if to say, "It's time to go home!"

I quickly loaded up the bike with our supplies. When I went back in to get Hoppy, he was gulping down his food and water. As soon as he finished, he hopped up onto my shoulder, anxious to head home. As we coasted along, I felt relieved. What was I thinking? How long could I have continued to lie to my parents, and how long did I think my friend and myself could continue such an existence? I remembered how happy he had been to escape our dark basement after his illness.

I decided not to tell my parents the whole story. What they didn't know wouldn't hurt them. When they saw Hoppy on my shoulder, they asked for details. I had to think fast. I told them that he was sitting on a fence which followed the road from my friend's house, and that when he recognized me, he instantly flew to my shoulder. Of course, he rode with me the rest of the way home.

I next told my dad about my cage ideas. I believed he was one of the smartest men in the world, especially when it came to knowing about pets and nature. Surely he could come up with some way that would enable us to keep my best friend. He told me he would think about it. Hoppy and I spent the rest of the day playing in the back yard. Of course, we had to play his favorite, bird-ball. And, as usual, he won! However, this was better than aggravating the neighbors. Our afternoon passed quickly. As I went inside to get ready for the school week, Hoppy flew up to his favorite branch outside my bedroom window.

CHAPTER 12

The next morning I noticed that Dad had a long face as I sat down to the breakfast table. He told me that he had been up most of the night trying to think of ways to keep Hoppy with us. However, he said that we had to do what was best for him, not us! A wild bird was meant to be free, not caged. Crows were mischievous and intelligent. How could Hoppy exercise these inherited traits if he were locked in a cage? He said that we could consider clipping my crow's wings, but he didn't think this would be in his best interest either. Hoppy would be unable to fly out of harm's way, and his lust for adventure would be extremely limited. If we took him off to a far away place and released him, he would be lonely and scared at first . . . But, he would be FREE.

    This choice broke my heart. I was still too young for these grown-up deductions. I went around in a daze. In fact, that is why two days later I fell in P.E. class during a tumbling session and badly sprained my leg. My teachers took me to the emergency room, where the doctor put me on crutches and ordered me not to walk for a week.

When I arrived home late that afternoon, an even greater misfortune awaited me. I hobbled around looking for Hoppy, but he was nowhere. He always swooped down to greet me the second I arrived home. I called out to him as I approached the front door. When I went inside, Mom said to stop calling. He was gone, forever. She told me that my dad had taken him far away to a big farm over in Illinois, where he released him to be with his own kind. The farmer was a friend of Dad's and agreed to leave food out for Hoppy and to look out for him.

All I can remember about that moment was wanting to run away to be with Hoppy, to try to find him. And I would have done just this, but I could not walk! I cried myself to sleep for nights to come, and had nightmares about what may have happened to my beloved crow for weeks, even months afterwards.

I never saw my most treasured friend again. The farmer reported to Dad that Hoppy disappeared a few days after his arrival. I have since often wondered how long he survived in that rural farmland, were he was released over fifty years ago. It is not uncommon for pet crows to live thirty years or longer. The life span of wild crows, however, is much shorter. These wild scavengers eat the crops of fields and gardens and thus have become a favorite target of the farmers' shotguns. Was Hoppy one of these targets?

Or, did he fly down to some other child's shoulder, bringing fun and joy to another family's home?

Or did he integrate with his own kind? Unfortunately, I have little hope that Hoppy found any solace with his fellow crows. I had often noticed that the wild crows, which hung around the open fields in back of our house, fussed and fumed at Hoppy every chance they got, swooping down and threatening him with angry "caws." Hoppy always ignored them. After all, he thought he was one of us, always trying to mimic our human tasks in every way he could, at work or play. Thus, it is easy to conclude that the wild crows probably chose to ostracize and taunt their domesticated brother, turning my beloved pet crow's release from captivity into an unhappy venture. How confused and frightened he must have been on that first day of his release. No wonder he soon flew off, probably seeking his home and best friend. Yes, Hoppy and I became best friends, but I would never again subject one of nature's wild creatures to his uncertain fate! Nevertheless, Dad always contended that this way at least he had a chance to be free. Then I remembered my best friend locked up in that dark old house, how he was overcome with gloom, and my heart told me that my dad must be right. He later apologized for bringing a wild creature home to me to keep as a pet, for he realized that the world had changed so much since his youth.

Oh, my Hoppy! I admired you more than anything in that twelfth year of my life. You brought such a sense of joy and adventure to my empty existence. Although the enormous pain of your loss was at first unbearable and filled me with pessimism and mistrust for years to come, memories of our special bond outshine the darkness. I miss you, still dream of you, and will love you always!